NFPA® 1033

Standard for

Professional Qualifications for Fire Investigator

2022 Edition

This edition of NFPA 1033, *Standard for Professional Qualifications for Fire Investigator*, was prepared by the Technical Committee on Fire Investigator Professional Qualifications and released by the Correlating Committee on Professional Qualifications. It was issued by the Standards Council on May 24, 2021, with an effective date of June 13, 2021, and supersedes all previous editions.

This edition of NFPA 1033 was approved as an American National Standard on June 13, 2021.

Origin and Development of NFPA 1033

In 1972, the Joint Council of National Fire Service Organizations (JCNFSO) created the National Professional Qualifications Board (NPQB) for the fire service to facilitate the development of nationally applicable performance standards for uniformed fire service personnel. On December 14, 1972, the board established four technical committees to develop those standards using the National Fire Protection Association (NFPA) standards-making system. The initial committees addressed the following career areas: fire fighter, fire officer, fire service instructor, and fire inspector and investigator.

The original concept of the professional qualification standards as directed by the JCNFSO and the NPQB was to develop an interrelated set of performance standards specifically for the uniformed fire service. The various levels of achievement in the standards were to build upon each other within a strictly defined career ladder. In the late 1980s, revisions of the standards recognized that the documents should stand on their own merit in terms of job performance requirements for a given field. Accordingly, the strict career ladder concept was revised, except for the progression from fire fighter to fire officer, in order to allow civilian entry into many of the fields. These revisions facilitated the use of the documents by other than the uniformed fire services. The Committee on Fire Inspector and Investigator Professional Qualifications met and produced the first edition of NFPA 1031, *Professional Qualifications for Fire Inspector, Fire Investigator, and Fire Prevention Education Officer*. This document was adopted by the NFPA in May of 1977.

In 1986, the joint council directed the committee to develop separate documents for each of the job functions the original document addressed. This direction was coupled with the decision to remove the job of fire investigator from the strict career path previously followed and allow for civilian entry. The first edition of this new document, NFPA 1033, *Standard for Professional Qualifications for Fire Investigator*, was adopted by the NFPA in June of 1987.

In 1990, responsibility for the appointment of professional qualifications committees and the development of the professional qualifications standards was assumed by the NFPA. The Professional Qualifications Correlating Committee was appointed by the NFPA Standards Council and assumed the responsibility for coordinating the requirements of all of the documents in the professional qualifications system.

The NFPA Standards Council established the Technical Committee on Fire Investigator Professional Qualifications in 1990 to address the need for specific expertise in the area of fire investigation to review and revise the existing document. This committee completed a job task analysis and developed specific job performance requirements for the job of fire investigator.

The intent of the Technical Committee on Fire Investigator Professional Qualifications was to develop clear and concise job performance requirements that can be used to determine that an individual, when measured to the standard, possesses the skills and knowledge to perform as a fire investigator. These job performance requirements are applicable to fire investigators both public and private.

In the 2003 edition of the document, the Technical Committee made changes to bring it into conformance with the new *Manual of Style for NFPA Technical Committee Documents*.

In the 2009 edition of the document, the Technical Committee added an explanatory annex item to the Scope statement. The committee's intent was to clarify that the standard applies to all fire investigation, including outside, vehicle, and other fires that are not structural. The committee added a skills maintenance requirement to Chapter 1 and included more specific Requisite Knowledge statements to various JPRs.

For the 2014 edition, the fire investigator was expected to remain current on the topics listed in the general requirements section of the document by attending formal education courses, workshops, and seminars, and through professional publications and journals. While the technical committee viewed a high-school level education as a minimum, the fire investigator was expected to maintain up-to-date basic knowledge of topics already projected in the document, as well as knowledge of fire protection systems; evidence documentation, collection, and preservation; and electricity and electric systems. Definitions for *fire analysis, fire dynamics, fire investigation technology*, and *fire science* were added. The technical committee also made clarifications under the evidence collection and preservation section of the document.

For the 2022 edition, the committee made several updates and changes throughout the document to align it more closely with NFPA 921, since it is common practice for fire investigators meeting NFPA 1033 to also use NFPA 921. The committee also updated and simplified requirements that had been a source of confusion for end users to make them easier to understand.

Correlating Committee on Professional Qualifications

William E. Peterson, *Chair*
Kissimmee, FL [M]
Rep. International Fire Service Training Association

Brian Baughman, Generac Power Systems Inc., WI [M]

Brian R. Brauer, University of Illinois Fire Service Institute, IL [E]
Rep. National Board on Fire Service Professional Qualifications

Derrick S. Clouston, North Carolina Department of Insurance, NC [U]

Gregory S. Cross, Texas A&M Engineer Extension Service, TX [SE]

Jason Dolf, Aerial Services Inc, IA [U]

Angus Maclean Duff, Consolidated Fire District 2, KS [U]

Richard A. Dunn, SC State Firefighters' Association, SC [E]

Alec Feldman, Fulcrum Consultants, Ireland [SE]
Rep. JOIFF-International Organisation for Industrial Hazard Management

Douglas P. Forsman, Fairfield Bay Fire Department, AR [L]

Richard Galtieri, Port Of Seattle Fire Department, WA [E]

Douglas R. Goodings, St. Clair Community College, Canada [SE]

Scott M. Gorgon, IAFF, DC [L]

R. Kirk Hankins, Fire Consulting & Case Review International, Inc., MO [U]
Rep. International Association of Arson Investigators, Inc.

Bill Slosson, Washington State Patrol, WA [E]

Philip C. Stittleburg, La Farge Fire Department, WI [L]
Rep. National Volunteer Fire Council

Matthew Brian Thorpe, North Carolina Office of the State Fire Marshal, NC [E]
Rep. International Fire Service Accreditation Congress

Charles "Randy" Watson, S-E-A, Ltd., GA [SE]

Michael J. Yurgec, Global Emergency Products, IL [M]

Alternates

Adam J. Goodman, S-E-A Limited, MD [SE]
(Alt. to Charles "Randy" Watson)

David W. Lewis, Odenton, MD [L]
(Alt. to Philip C. Stittleburg)

Robert W. Rand, Nat'l Board On Fire Service Prof. Qualifications, MA [E]
(Alt. to Brian R. Brauer)

Angela White, Wisconsin Technical College System, WI [E]
(Alt. to Matthew Brian Thorpe)

Nonvoting

Stephen P. Austin, Cumberland Valley Volunteer Firemen's Association, DE [L]
Rep. TC on Traffic Control Incident Management Professional Qualifications

Preet Bassi, Center For Public Safety Excellence, VA [C]
Rep. TC on Fire Service Analysts and Informational Technical Specialist

Alan W. Conkle, Ohio Association of Emergency Vehicle Technicians (OAEVT), OH [M]
Rep. TC on Emergency Vehicle Mechanic Technicians Professional Qualifications

John S. Cunningham, Nova Scotia Firefighters School, Canada [U]
Rep. TC on Fire Fighter Professional Qualifications

Jay Dornseif, III, Priority Dispatch Corporation, UT [M]
Rep. TC on Public Safety Telecommunicator Professional Qualifications

Richard C. Edinger, Chester, VA [SE]
Rep. TC on Hazardous Materials Response Personnel

Ronald R. Farr, Plainwell Fire Department, MI [C]
Rep. TC on Electrical Inspection Practices

Dave E. Hanneman, Self Employed, ID [SE]
Rep. TC on Incident Management Professional Qualifications

Daniel P. Heenan, Clark County Fire Department, NV [E]
Rep. TC on Fire Investigator Professional Qualifications

Orlando P. Hernandez, Texas State Fire Marshal's Office, TX [E]
Rep. TC on Rescue Technician Professional Qualifications

Ronald L. Hopkins, TRACE Fire Protection & Safety Consultant, Ltd., KY [SE]
Rep. TC on Fire Service Instructor Professional Qualifications

Robert J. James, UL LLC, IL [RT]
Rep. TC on Building Fire and Life Safety Director Professional Qualifications

Randy J. Krause, Port of Seattle Fire Department, WA [E]
Rep. TC on Fire Service Occupational Safety and Health

Peter J. Mulvihill, Reno, NV [SE]
Rep. TC on Fire Inspector Professional Qualifications

Randal E. Novak, Ames, IA [SE]
Rep. TC on Accreditation & Certification Professional Qualifications

Lawrence L. Preston, Maryland Fire and Rescue Institute, MD [E]
Rep. TC on Fire Officer Professional Qualifications

Jim Stumpf, Organizational Quality Associates, ID [SE]
Rep. TC on Wildfire Suppression Professional Qualifications

Robert D. Taylor, PRB Coal Users Group, IN [U]
Rep. TC on Industrial Fire Brigades Professional Qualifications

Nancy J. Trench, Stillwater, OK [M]
Rep. TC on Public Fire Educator Professional Qualifications

Paul Valentine, TUV SUD America Inc./Global Risk Consultants, IL [M]
Rep. TC on Fire Marshal Professional Qualifications

Robert Fash, NFPA Staff Liaison

This list represents the membership at the time the Committee was balloted on the final text of this edition. Since that time, changes in the membership may have occurred. A key to classifications is found at the back of the document.

NOTE: Membership on a committee shall not in and of itself constitute an endorsement of the Association or any document developed by the committee on which the member serves.

Committee Scope: This Committee shall have primary responsibility for the management of the NFPA Professional Qualifications Project and documents related to professional qualifications for fire service, public safety, and related personnel.

Technical Committee on Fire Investigator Professional Qualifications

Daniel P. Heenan, *Chair*
Clark County Fire Department, NV [E]

Mark A. Beavers, Travelers Insurance, VA [I]

Adrian J. Cales, Public Service Enterprise Group, NJ [U]

Steve Campolo, Leviton Manufacturing Company, Inc., NY [M]
Rep. National Electrical Manufacturers Association

Karrie J. Clinkinbeard, Armstrong Teasdale LLP, MO [U]

Kevin T. Dippolito, Township of Bristol, Fire Marshal, PA [U]

Dennis Field, Fire Cause Analysis, CA [SE]

Gregory E. Gorbett, Eastern Kentucky University, KY [SE]

Todd M. Iaeger, UL LLC, PA [RT]

Todd Kerkhoff, Consolidated Fire District #2, KS [U]

John C. Kernan, Upper Makefield Township Fire Marshal, PA [E]

Kelly Kistner, Forensic Investigations Group, LLC, TX [E]

Roger A. Krupp, Clarendon Hills Fire Department, IL [U]
Rep. International Association of Arson Investigators, Inc.

John J. Lentini, Scientific Fire Analysis, LLC, FL [SE]

Kevin Lewis, JENSEN HUGHES, WA [SE]

Joseph T. Lombardi, Connecticut State Police, CT [E]

Wayne J. McKenna, McKenna Hewitt, CO [SE]

David W. Miller, Grinnell Mutual Reinsurance Company, IA [I]

Richard E. Morris, REMCo Fire Investigations, CT [U]

Gerard J. Naylis, Technical Fire Services, Inc., NJ [SE]

Devin J. Palmer, US Bureau of Alcohol, Tobacco, Firearms & Explosives (ATF), IL [U]

Stuart A. Sklar, Fabian, Sklar and King, P.C., MI [U]

Dennis W. Smith, Premier Fire Consulting Services, LLC, FL [SE]

G. Terry Smith, EFI Global, IA [SE]

Nicholas James Smith, Pyr-tech Fire & Explosion Experts, MO [U]
Rep. National Association of Fire Investigators

Jason Wallace, S-E-A, Ltd., OH [SE]

Steve Young, Wolf Creek Fire Department/Travelers Insurance, MO [E]

Alternates

Kevin L. Dunkin, Grinnell Mutual Reinsurance Company, MO [I]
(Alt. to David W. Miller)

Mark Goodson, Goodson Engineering, TX [SE]
(Alt. to John J. Lentini)

Ricky A. Hankins, US Bureau of Alcohol, Tobacco, Firearms & Explosives (ATF), WI [U]
(Alt. to Devin J. Palmer)

Terry-Dawn Hewitt, McKenna Hewitt, CO [SE]
(Alt. to Wayne J. McKenna)

William D. Hicks, Eastern Kentucky University, KY [SE]
(Alt. to Gregory E. Gorbett)

Gerald A. King, Armstrong Teasdale LLP, MO [U]
(Alt. to Karrie J. Clinkinbeard)

Jason J. Liss, Fabian, Sklar and King, P.C., MI [U]
(Alt. to Stuart A. Sklar)

Hal C. Lyson, Fire Cause Analysis, ND [SE]
(Alt. to Dennis Field)

Michael S. O'Boyle, Philips Lightolier/Signify North America Corp., MA [M]
(Alt. to Steve Campolo)

Andrew Paris, JENSEN HUGHES, WA [SE]
(Alt. to Kevin Lewis)

James H. Shanley, Jr., Travelers Insurance Company, CT [I]
(Alt. to Mark A. Beavers)

Kathryn C. Smith, National Association of Fire Investigators, FL [U]
(Alt. to Nicholas James Smith)

Jack A. Ward, Jack Ward Fire Consultants, LLC, FL [U]
(Alt. to Roger A. Krupp)

Charles "Randy" Watson, S-E-A, Ltd., GA [SE]
(Alt. to Jason Wallace)

David A. Wilson, Engineering Systems Inc., NC [SE]
(Alt. to Dennis W. Smith)

Nonvoting

Michael L. Donahue, US Department of Homeland Security, MD [U]

Ken Holland, NFPA Staff Liaison

This list represents the membership at the time the Committee was balloted on the final text of this edition. Since that time, changes in the membership may have occurred. A key to classifications is found at the back of the document.

NOTE: Membership on a committee shall not in and of itself constitute an endorsement of the Association or any document developed by the committee on which the member serves.

Committee Scope: This Committee shall have primary responsibility for documents on professional qualifications required of fire investigators.

Contents

NFPA 1033

Standard for

Professional Qualifications for Fire Investigator

2022 Edition

IMPORTANT NOTE: This NFPA document is made available for use subject to important notices and legal disclaimers. These notices and disclaimers appear in all publications containing this document and may be found under the heading "Important Notices and Disclaimers Concerning NFPA Standards." They can also be viewed at www.nfpa.org/disclaimers or obtained on request from NFPA.

UPDATES, ALERTS, AND FUTURE EDITIONS: New editions of NFPA codes, standards, recommended practices, and guides (i.e., NFPA Standards) are released on scheduled revision cycles. This edition may be superseded by a later one, or it may be amended outside of its scheduled revision cycle through the issuance of Tentative Interim Amendments (TIAs). An official NFPA Standard at any point in time consists of the current edition of the document, together with all TIAs and Errata in effect. To verify that this document is the current edition or to determine if it has been amended by TIAs or Errata, please consult the National Fire Codes® Subscription Service or the "List of NFPA Codes & Standards" at www.nfpa.org/docinfo. In addition to TIAs and Errata, the document information pages also include the option to sign up for alerts for individual documents and to be involved in the development of the next edition.

NOTICE: An asterisk (*) following the number or letter designating a paragraph indicates that explanatory material on the paragraph can be found in Annex A.

A reference in brackets [ ] following a section or paragraph indicates material that has been extracted from another NFPA document. Extracted text may be edited for consistency and style and may include the revision of internal paragraph references and other references as appropriate. Requests for interpretations or revisions of extracted text shall be sent to the technical committee responsible for the source document.

Information on referenced and extracted publications can be found in Chapter 2 and Annex E.

Chapter 1 Administration

1.1* Scope. This standard shall identify the minimum job performance requirements (JPRs) for fire investigators.

1.2* Purpose. This standard shall specify the minimum JPRs for serving as a fire investigator in both the private and public sectors.

1.2.1 This standard shall define the fire investigator position.

1.2.2 The intent of this standard shall be to ensure that individuals who serve as fire investigators are qualified to do so.

1.2.3 It shall not be the intent of this standard to restrict any jurisdiction from exceeding or combining these minimum requirements.

1.2.4 JPRs for each duty are the tasks personnel shall be able to perform to successfully carry out that duty.

1.2.5 Fire investigators who perform or support fire investigations shall remain current with the general knowledge, skills, and JPRs.

1.2.6 Fire investigators who perform or support fire investigations shall remain current with practices and applicable standards.

1.3 Application. The application of this standard shall be to specify the JPRs that shall apply to specific personnel who perform and support fire investigations.

1.3.1 The JPRs shall be accomplished in accordance with the requirements of the AHJ and all applicable NFPA and other standards development organization (SDO) standards.

1.3.2 Priority.

1.3.2.1* It shall not be required that the JPRs be mastered in the order in which they appear.

1.3.2.2 The AHJ shall establish instructional priority and the training program content to prepare personnel to meet the JPRs of this standard.

1.3.2.3* The performance of each requirement of this chapter shall be evaluated by personnel approved by the AHJ.

1.3.2.4 The JPRs for fire investigators shall be completed in accordance with recognized practices and procedures or as defined by law or by the AHJ.

1.3.2.5 Fire investigators who perform or support fire investigations shall meet the requirements of this standard for each fire investigation performed.

1.3.2.6 The AHJ shall provide the necessary personal protective equipment (PPE), force protection, and clothing to conduct assignments.

1.3.2.7 JPRs involving exposure to products of combustion shall be performed in approved PPE.

1.3.2.8 Prior to training to meet the requirements of this standard, personnel shall meet the following requirements:

(1) Be at least age 18
(2) Have a high school diploma or equivalent
(3) Be subjected to a thorough background and character investigation by the AHJ prior to being accepted as an individual candidate for certification as a fire investigator

Chapter 2 Referenced Publications

2.1 General. The documents or portions thereof listed in this chapter are referenced within this standard and shall be considered part of the requirements of this document.

2.2 NFPA Publications. (Reserved)

2.3 Other Publications.

Merriam-Webster's Collegiate Dictionary, 11th edition, Merriam-Webster, Inc., Springfield, MA, 2003.

2.4 References for Extracts in Mandatory Sections.

NFPA *101*®, *Life Safety Code*®, 2021 edition.
NFPA 901, *Standard Classifications for Incident Reporting and Fire Protection Data*, 2021 edition.

NFPA 921, *Guide for Fire and Explosion Investigations*, 2021 edition.

NFPA 1031, *Standard for Professional Qualifications for Fire Inspector and Plan Examiner*, 2014 edition.

Chapter 3 Definitions

3.1 General. The definitions contained in this chapter shall apply to the terms used in this standard. Where terms are not defined in this chapter or within another chapter, they shall be defined using their ordinarily accepted meanings within the context in which they are used. *Merriam-Webster's Collegiate Dictionary*, 11th edition, shall be the source for the ordinarily accepted meaning.

3.2 NFPA Official Definitions.

3.2.1* Approved. Acceptable to the authority having jurisdiction.

3.2.2* Authority Having Jurisdiction (AHJ). An organization, office, or individual responsible for enforcing the requirements of a code or standard, or for approving equipment, materials, an installation, or a procedure.

3.2.3 Labeled. Equipment or materials to which has been attached a label, symbol, or other identifying mark of an organization that is acceptable to the authority having jurisdiction and concerned with product evaluation, that maintains periodic inspection of production of labeled equipment or materials, and by whose labeling the manufacturer indicates compliance with appropriate standards or performance in a specified manner.

3.2.4* Listed. Equipment, materials, or services included in a list published by an organization that is acceptable to the authority having jurisdiction and concerned with evaluation of products or services, that maintains periodic inspection of production of listed equipment or materials or periodic evaluation of services, and whose listing states that either the equipment, material, or service meets appropriate designated standards or has been tested and found suitable for a specified purpose.

3.2.5 Shall. Indicates a mandatory requirement.

3.2.6 Should. Indicates a recommendation or that which is advised but not required.

3.2.7 Standard. An NFPA Standard, the main text of which contains only mandatory provisions using the word "shall" to indicate requirements and that is in a form generally suitable for mandatory reference by another standard or code or for adoption into law. Nonmandatory provisions are not to be considered a part of the requirements of a standard and shall be located in an appendix, annex, footnote, informational note, or other means as permitted in the NFPA Manuals of Style. When used in a generic sense, such as in the phrase "standards development process" or "standards development activities," the term "standards" includes all NFPA Standards, including Codes, Standards, Recommended Practices, and Guides.

3.3 General Definitions.

3.3.1 Due Process. The compliance with the criminal and civil laws and procedures within the jurisdiction where the incident occurred.

N **3.3.2 Explosion Dynamics.** Study of how chemistry, physics, fire science, engineering disciplines of fluid and solid mechanics, and heat transfer interact to influence explosion behavior. [**921**, 2021]

N **3.3.3 Failure Analysis.** A logical, systematic examination of an item, component, assembly, or structure and its place and function within a system, conducted in order to identify and analyze the probability, causes, and consequences of potential and real failures. [**921**, 2021]

3.3.4 Fire Analysis. The process of determining the origin, cause, development, responsibility, and, when required, a failure analysis of a fire or explosion. [**921, 2021**]

N **3.3.5 Fire Chemistry.** The study of chemical processes that occur in fires including changes in state, decomposition, and combustion. [**921**, 2021]

3.3.6 Fire Department. An organization providing rescue, fire suppression, and related activities. For the purposes of this standard, the term "fire department" includes any public, private, or military organization engaging in this type of activity.

3.3.7 Fire Dynamics. The detailed study of how chemistry, fire science, and the engineering disciplines of fluid mechanics and heat transfer interact to influence fire behavior. [**921, 2021**]

3.3.8 Fire Investigation. The process of determining the origin, cause, and development of a fire or explosion. [**921, 2021**]

3.3.9 Fire Investigation Technology. Applied technology subjects related to and used in fire investigation including, but not limited to, specialized knowledge and skills in documentation of the investigation, scene and evidence processing, and failure analysis and analytical tools.

3.3.10 Fire Investigator. An individual who has demonstrated the skills and knowledge necessary to conduct, coordinate, and complete a fire investigation.

N **3.3.11 Fire Model.** A structured approach to predicting one or more effects of a fire. [*101*, 2021]

N **3.3.12 Fire Protection Systems.** Systems, devices, and equipment used to detect a fire and its by-products, actuate an alarm, or suppress or control a fire and its by-products, or any combination thereof. [**1031**, 2014]

3.3.13 Fire Science. The body of knowledge concerning the study of fire and related subjects (such as combustion, flame, products of combustion, heat release, heat transfer, fire and explosion chemistry, fire and explosion dynamics, thermodynamics, kinetics, fluid mechanics, fire safety) and their interaction with people, structures, and the environment. [**921, 2021**]

N **3.3.14 Fuel Gas.** Natural gas, manufactured gas, LP-Gas, and similar gases commonly used for commercial or residential purposes such as heating, cooling, or cooking. [**921**, 2021]

N **3.3.15 Hazardous Materials.** Any material that is an air-reactive material, flammable or combustible liquid, flammable gas, corrosive material, explosive material, organic peroxide, oxidizing material, radioactive material, toxic material, unstable material, biological material or water-reactive material, and any substance or mixture of substances that is an irritant or a strong sensitizer or that generates pressure through exposure to heat, decomposition, or other means. [**901**, 2021]

3.3.16 Heat Transfer. The exchange of thermal energy between materials through conduction, convection, and/or radiation. [**921, 2021**]

3.3.17 Job Performance Requirement. A statement that describes a specific job task, lists the items necessary to complete the task, and defines measurable or observable outcomes and evaluation areas for the specific task.

3.3.18 Requisite Knowledge. Fundamental knowledge one must have in order to perform a specific task.

3.3.19 Requisite Skills. The essential skills one must have in order to perform a specific task.

3.3.20 Task. A specific job behavior or activity.

3.3.21 Tools.

3.3.21.1* *Investigator's Special Tools.* Tools of a specialized or unique nature that might not be required for every fire investigation.

3.3.21.2* *Standard Equipment and Tools.* Investigator's tools and equipment that every investigator must carry.

Chapter 4   Fire Investigator

4.1 General.

4.1.1* The fire investigator shall meet the job performance requirements (JPRs) defined in Sections 4.2 through 4.7.

4.1.2* The fire investigator shall employ all elements of the scientific method as the operating analytical process throughout the investigation and for the drawing of conclusions.

4.1.3* Because fire investigators are required to perform activities in adverse conditions, site safety assessments shall be completed on all scenes and regional and national safety standards shall be followed and included in organizational policies and procedures.

4.1.4* The fire investigator shall maintain necessary liaison with other interested professionals and entities.

4.1.5* The fire investigator shall adhere to all applicable legal and regulatory requirements.

4.1.6 The fire investigator shall understand the organization and operation of the investigative team within an incident management system.

4.1.7* In order to successfully complete the tasks identified in the JPRs of Sections 4.2 through 4.7, the fire investigator shall remain current in the subjects listed as "requisite knowledge" as they relate to fire investigations, which include the following:

(1) Fire science:

   (a) Fire chemistry
   (b) Thermodynamics
   (c) Fire dynamics
   (d) Explosion dynamics

(2) Fire investigation:

   (a) Fire analysis
   (b) Fire investigation methodology
   (c) Fire investigation technology
   (d) Evidence documentation, collection, and preservation

   (e) Failure analysis and analytical tools

(3) Fire scene safety:

   (a) Hazard recognition, evaluation, and basic mitigation procedures
   (b) Hazardous materials
   (c) Safety regulations

(4) Building systems:

   (a) Types of construction
   (b) Fire protection systems
   (c) Electricity and electrical systems
   (d) Fuel gas systems

N 4.1.7.1 The fire investigator shall remain current in the subjects listed as "requisite knowledge" for the JPRs and as summarized in 4.1.7.

N 4.1.7.2 The fire investigator shall remain current by attending formal education courses, workshops, in-person or online seminars, and/or through professional publications, journals, and treatises.

N 4.1.7.3 The fire investigator shall complete and document a minimum of 40 hours of continuing education training every five years by attending formal education courses, workshops, and seminars.

Δ 4.2* Scene Examination. Duties shall include inspecting, evaluating, and analyzing the fire scene or evidence of the scene, and conducting a comprehensive review of documentation generated during the examination(s) of the scene if the scene is no longer available, so as to determine the area or point of origin, source of ignition, material(s) ignited, and action or activity that brought the ignition source and materials together and to assess the subsequent progression, extinguishment, and containment of the fire.

4.2.1 Secure the fire ground, given marking devices, sufficient personnel, and special tools and equipment, so that unauthorized persons can recognize the perimeters of the investigative scene and are kept from restricted areas and all evidence or potential evidence is protected from damage or destruction.

(A) Requisite Knowledge. Fire ground hazards, types of evidence, and the importance of fire scene security, evidence preservation, and issues relating to spoliation.

(B) Requisite Skills. Use of marking devices.

4.2.2* Conduct an exterior survey, given standard equipment and tools, so that evidence is identified and preserved, fire damage is interpreted and analyzed, hazards are identified to avoid injuries, accessibility to the property is determined, and all potential means of ingress and egress are discovered.

(A) Requisite Knowledge. The types of building construction and the effects of fire on construction materials, types of evidence commonly found in the perimeter, evidence preservation methods, the effects of fire suppression, fire behavior and spread, fire patterns, and a basic awareness of the dangers of hazardous materials.

(B) Requisite Skills. Ability to assess fire ground and structural condition, observe the damage from and effects of the fire, and interpret and analyze fire patterns.

4.2.3 Conduct an interior survey, given standard equipment and tools, so that areas of potential evidentiary value requiring further examination are identified and preserved, the evidentiary value of contents is determined, and hazards are identified in order to avoid injuries.

(A) Requisite Knowledge. The types of building construction and interior finish and the effects of fire on those materials, the effects of fire suppression, fire behavior and spread, evidence preservation methods, fire patterns, effects of building contents on fire growth, the relationship of building contents to the overall investigation, weather conditions at the time of the fire, and fuel moisture.

(B) Requisite Skills. Ability to assess structural conditions, observe the damage and effects of the fire, discover the impact of fire suppression efforts on fire flow and heat propagation, and evaluate protected areas to determine the presence and/or absence of contents.

△ **4.2.4** Interpret and analyze fire patterns, given standard equipment and tools and some structural or content remains, so that each pattern is identified and analyzed with respect to the burning characteristics of the material involved, the stage of fire development, the effects of ventilation within the context of the scene, the relationship with all patterns observed, and the understanding of the methods of heat transfer that led to the formation of the patterns identified and analyzed, and the sequence in which the patterns were produced is determined.

(A) Requisite Knowledge. Fire dynamics, including stages of fire development; methods of heat transfer; compartment fire development; the interrelationship of heat release rate (HRR), form, and ignitibility of materials; and the impact and effects of ventilation on the creation of the fire patterns.

(B) Requisite Skills. Ability to interpret and analyze the effects of burning characteristics of the fuel involved and the effects of ventilation on different types of materials.

4.2.5 Interpret and analyze fire patterns, given standard equipment and tools and some structural or content remains, so that fire development, fire spread, and the sequence in which fire patterns were developed (i.e., sequential pattern analysis) are determined; methods and effects of suppression are analyzed; fire patterns and effects indicating a hypothetical area or areas of origin are recognized and tested; false or refuted hypothetical areas of origin are eliminated; and all fire patterns are tested against the data, such that the area(s) of origin is correctly identified.

(A) Requisite Knowledge. Fire development and spread based on fire chemistry, fire dynamics including compartment fire development, fire spread, fire suppression effects, building construction, electricity and electrical systems, and fuel gas systems.

(B) Requisite Skills. Ability to analyze variations of fire patterns on different materials with consideration given to HRR, form, ignitibility of the fuels involved, and the effects of ventilation; ability to understand the impact of different types of fuel packages on pattern creation; and ability to analyze and correlate information.

4.2.6 Examine and remove fire debris, given standard or, if necessary, special equipment and tools, so that fire patterns and fire effects concealed by debris are discovered and analyzed; all debris within the potential area(s) of origin is checked for fire cause evidence; potential ignition source(s) is

identified; and evidence is preserved without investigator inflicted damage or contamination.

(A) Requisite Knowledge. Basic understanding of ignition processes, characteristics of ignition sources, and ease of ignition of fuels; debris-layering techniques; use of tools, equipment, and special equipment during the debris search; types of fire cause evidence commonly found; understanding evidence spoliation and techniques to avoid it; and evidence collection and preservation methods and documentation.

(B) Requisite Skills. Ability to employ search techniques that further the discovery of fire cause evidence and ignition sources, use search techniques that incorporate documentation, and collect and preserve evidence.

△ **4.2.7** Reconstruct potential area(s) of origin, given standard and, if needed, special equipment and tools as well as sufficient personnel, so that all protected areas and fire patterns are identified and correlated to contents or structural remains; and items potentially critical to cause determination are returned to their prefire location as a means of hypothesis testing, such that the area(s) or point(s) of origin is discovered.

(A) Requisite Knowledge. The effects of fire on different types of material and the importance and uses of reconstruction.

(B) Requisite Skills. Ability to examine all materials to determine the effects of fire, identify and distinguish among different types of fire-damaged contents, and return materials to their original position using protected areas and fire patterns.

△ **4.2.8*** Inspect and analyze the performance of building systems, including fire protection, detection and suppression systems, HVAC, electricity and electrical systems, fuel gas systems, and building compartmentation, given standard and special equipment and tools, so that a determination can be made as to the need for expert resources; an operating system's impact on fire growth and spread is considered in identifying origin areas; defeated and failed systems are identified; and the system's potential as a fire cause is recognized.

(A) Requisite Knowledge. Different types of fire protection, detection, suppression, HVAC, electricity and electrical systems, fuel gas systems, and building compartmentation such as fire walls and fire doors; types of expert resources for building systems; the impact of fire on various systems; common methods used to defeat a system's functional capability; and types of failures.

(B) Requisite Skills. Ability to determine the system's operation and its effect on the fire; identify alterations to, and failure indicators of, building systems; and evaluate the impact of suppression efforts on building systems.

4.2.9 Discriminate the effects of explosions from other types of damage, given standard equipment and tools, so that an explosion is identified and its evidence is preserved.

(A) Requisite Knowledge. Different types of explosions and their causes, characteristics of an explosion, and the difference between low- and high-order explosions.

(B) Requisite Skills. Ability to identify explosive effects on glass, walls, foundations, and other building materials; distinguish between low- and high-order explosion effects; and analyze damage to document the blast zone and origin.

Shaded text = Revisions. △ = Text deletions and figure/table revisions. • = Section deletions. **N** = New material.

4.3 Documenting the Scene. Duties shall include diagramming the scene, photographing, and taking field notes to be used to document scene findings, or to prepare a written report.

4.3.1 Diagram the scene, given standard tools and equipment, so that the scene is accurately represented and evidence, pertinent contents, significant patterns, and area(s) or point(s) of origin are identified.

(A) Requisite Knowledge. Commonly used symbols and legends that clarify the diagram, types of evidence and patterns that need to be documented, and formats for diagramming the scene.

(B) Requisite Skills. Ability to sketch the scene, basic drafting skills, and evidence recognition and observational skills.

4.3.2* Photographically document the scene, given standard tools and equipment, so that the scene is accurately depicted and the photographs support scene findings.

(A) Requisite Knowledge. Working knowledge of high-resolution camera and flash, the types of film, media, and flash available, and the strengths and limitations of each.

(B) Requisite Skills. Ability to use a high-resolution camera, flash, and accessories.

4.3.3* Construct investigative notes, given a fire scene, available documents (e.g., prefire plans and inspection reports), and interview information, so that the notes are accurate, provide further documentation of the scene, and represent complete documentation of the scene findings.

(A) Requisite Knowledge. Relationship between notes, diagrams, and photos; how to reduce scene information into concise notes; and the use of notes during report writing and legal proceedings.

(B) Requisite Skills. Data-reduction skills, note-taking skills, and observational and correlating skills.

4.4 Evidence Collection/Preservation. Duties shall include using proper physical and legal procedures to identify, document, collect, and preserve evidence required within the investigation.

4.4.1 Utilize proper procedures for managing victims and fatalities, given a protocol and appropriate personnel, so that all evidence is discovered and preserved and the protocol procedures are followed.

(A) Requisite Knowledge. Types of evidence associated with fire victims and fatalities and evidence preservation methods.

(B) Requisite Skills. Observational skills and the ability to apply protocols to given situations.

4.4.2* Locate, document, collect, label, package, and store evidence, given standard or special tools and equipment and evidence collection materials, so that evidence is properly identified, preserved, collected, packaged, and stored for use in testing, legal, or other proceedings and examinations; ensuring cross-contamination and investigator-inflicted damage to evidentiary items are avoided; and the chain of custody is established.

(A) Requisite Knowledge. Types of evidence, authority requirements, and impact of removing evidentiary items on civil or criminal proceedings (exclusionary or fire-cause

supportive evidence); types, capabilities, and limitations of standard and special tools used to locate evidence; types of laboratory tests available; packaging techniques and materials; and impact of evidence collection on the investigation.

(B) Requisite Skills. Ability to recognize different types of evidence and determine whether evidence is critical to the investigation.

4.4.3 Select evidence for analysis, given all information from the investigation, so that items for analysis support specific investigation needs.

(A) Requisite Knowledge. Purposes for submitting items for analysis, types of analytical services available, and capabilities and limitations of the services performing the analysis.

(B) Requisite Skills. Ability to evaluate the fire incident to determine forensic, engineering, or laboratory needs.

4.4.4 Maintain a chain of custody, given standard investigative tools, marking tools, and evidence tags or logs, so that written documentation exists for each piece of evidence and evidence is secured.

(A) Requisite Knowledge. Rules of custody and transfer procedures, types of evidence (e.g., physical evidence obtained at the scene, photos, and documents), and methods of recording the chain of custody.

(B) Requisite Skills. Ability to execute the chain of custody procedures and accurately complete necessary documents.

4.4.5 Dispose of evidence, given jurisdictional or agency regulations and file information, so that the disposal is timely, safely conducted, and in compliance with jurisdictional or agency requirements.

(A) Requisite Knowledge. Disposal services available and common disposal procedures and problems.

(B) Requisite Skills. Documentation skills.

4.5 Interview. Duties shall include obtaining information regarding the overall fire investigation from others through verbal communication.

4.5.1 Develop an interview plan, given no special tools or equipment, so that the plan reflects a strategy to further determine the fire cause and affix responsibility and includes a relevant questioning strategy for each individual to be interviewed that promotes the efficient use of the investigator's time.

(A) Requisite Knowledge. Persons who can provide information that furthers the fire cause determination or the affixing of responsibility, types of questions that are pertinent and efficient to ask of different information sources (first responders, neighbors, witnesses, suspects, and so forth), and pros and cons of interviews versus document gathering.

(B) Requisite Skills. Planning skills, development of focused questions for specific individuals, and evaluation of existing file data to help develop questions and fill investigative gaps.

4.5.2 Conduct interviews, given incident information, so that pertinent information is obtained, follow-up questions are asked, responses to all questions are elicited, and the response to each question is documented accurately.

(A) Requisite Knowledge. Types of interviews, personal information needed for proper documentation or follow-up, documenting methods and tools, and types of nonverbal communications and their meaning.

△ **(B) Requisite Skills.** Ability to adjust interviewing strategies based on deductive reasoning, interpret and analyze verbal and nonverbal communications, apply appropriate legal requirements, and exhibit strong listening skills.

4.5.3 Evaluate interview information, given interview transcripts or notes and incident data, so that all interview data is individually analyzed and correlated with all other interviews, corroborative and conflictive information is documented, and new leads are developed.

(A) Requisite Knowledge. Types of interviews, report evaluation methods, and data correlation methods.

(B) Requisite Skills. Data correlation skills and the ability to evaluate source information (e.g., first responders and other witnesses).

4.6 Post-Incident Investigation. Duties shall include the investigation of all factors beyond the fire scene at the time of the origin and cause determination.

4.6.1 Gather reports and records, given no special tools, equipment, or materials, so that all gathered documents are applicable to the investigation, complete, and authentic; the chain of custody is maintained; and the material is admissible in a legal proceeding.

(A) Requisite Knowledge. Types of reports needed that facilitate determining responsibility for the fire (e.g., police reports, fire reports, insurance policies, financial records, deeds, private investigator reports, outside photos, and videos) and location of these reports.

(B) Requisite Skills. Ability to identify the reports and documents necessary for the investigation, implement the chain of custody, and organizational skills.

4.6.2 Evaluate the investigative file, given all available file information, so that areas for further investigation are identified, the relationship between gathered documents and information is interpreted, and corroborative evidence and information discrepancies are discovered.

(A) Requisite Knowledge. File assessment and/or evaluation methods, including accurate documentation practices, and requisite investigative elements.

(B) Requisite Skills. Information assessment, correlation, and organizational skills.

4.6.3 Coordinate expert resources, given the investigative file, reports, and documents, so that the expert's competencies are matched to the specific investigation needs, financial expenditures are justified, and utilization clearly furthers the investigative goals of determining cause or affixing responsibility.

(A) Requisite Knowledge. How to assess one's own expertise, qualification to be called for expert testimony, types of expert resources (e.g., forensic, CPA, polygraph, financial, human behavior disorders, and engineering), and methods to identify expert resources.

(B) Requisite Skills. Ability to apply expert resources to further the investigation by networking with other investigators to identify experts, questioning experts relative to their qualifi-

cations, and developing a utilization plan for use of expert resources.

4.6.4 Establish evidence as to motive and/or opportunity, given an incendiary fire, so that the evidence is supported by documentation and meets the evidentiary requirements of the jurisdiction.

(A) Requisite Knowledge. Types of motives common to incendiary fires, methods used to discover opportunity, and human behavioral patterns relative to fire-setting.

(B) Requisite Skills. Financial analysis, records gathering and analysis, interviewing, and interpreting and analyzing fire scene information and evidence for relationship to motive and/or opportunity.

4.6.5* Formulate an opinion concerning origin, cause, or responsibility for the fire, given all investigative findings, so that the opinion regarding origin, cause, or responsibility for a fire is supported by the data, facts, records, reports, documents, scientific references, and evidence.

(A) Requisite Knowledge. Analytical methods and procedures (e.g., hypothesis development and testing, systems analysis, time lines, link analysis, fault tree analysis, and data reduction matrixing).

(B) Requisite Skills. Analytical and assimilation skills.

4.7 Presentations. Duties shall include the presentation of findings to those individuals not involved in the actual investigations.

△ **4.7.1*** Prepare a written report, given investigative findings, so that the report accurately reflects the facts, data, and scientific principles on which the investigator relied; clearly identifies and expresses the investigator's opinions and conclusions; and contains the reasoning by which each opinion or conclusion was reached in order to meet the requirements of the intended audience(s).

(A) Requisite Knowledge. Elements of writing, typical components of a written report, and types of audiences and their respective needs or requirements.

(B) Requisite Skills. Writing skills, ability to analyze information, and determine the reader's needs or requirements.

4.7.2 Express investigative findings verbally, given investigative findings, notes, a time allotment, and a specific audience, so that the information is accurate, the presentation is completed within the allotted time, and the presentation includes only need-to-know information for the intended audience.

(A) Requisite Knowledge. Types of investigative findings, the informational needs of various types of audiences, and the impact of releasing information.

(B) Requisite Skills. Communication skills and ability to determine audience needs and correlate findings.

4.7.3 Testify during legal proceedings, given investigative findings, so that the testimony accurately reflects the facts, data, and scientific principles on which the investigator relied; clearly identifies and expresses the investigator's opinions and conclusions; and contains the reasoning by which each opinion or conclusion was reached.

(A) Requisite Knowledge. Types of investigative findings, types of legal proceedings, professional demeanor requirements, and an understanding of due process and legal proceedings.

(B) Requisite Skills. Communication and listening skills and ability to differentiate facts from opinion and determine accepted procedures, practices, and etiquette during legal proceedings.

Annex A Explanatory Material

Annex A is not a part of the requirements of this NFPA document but is included for informational purposes only. This annex contains explanatory material, numbered to correspond with the applicable text paragraphs.

A.1.1 The intent of this standard applies to all fire investigation, including outside, wildland, vehicle, and structural fires.

A.1.2 See Annex B.

A.1.3.2.1 See Annex B.

A.1.3.2.3 Those responsible for conducting evaluations should have experience levels or qualifications exceeding those being evaluated or be certified as a fire investigator by an accredited agency, and be trained or qualified to conduct performance evaluations. The latter, for AHJs, can be based on instructor certification. Many agencies select specialists to evaluate various sections of Chapter 4, which the committee accepts as best practice.

A.3.2.1 Approved. The National Fire Protection Association does not approve, inspect, or certify any installations, procedures, equipment, or materials; nor does it approve or evaluate testing laboratories. In determining the acceptability of installations, procedures, equipment, or materials, the authority having jurisdiction may base acceptance on compliance with NFPA or other appropriate standards. In the absence of such standards, said authority may require evidence of proper installation, procedure, or use. The authority having jurisdiction may also refer to the listings or labeling practices of an organization that is concerned with product evaluations and is thus in a position to determine compliance with appropriate standards for the current production of listed items.

A.3.2.2 Authority Having Jurisdiction (AHJ). The phrase "authority having jurisdiction," or its acronym AHJ, is used in NFPA documents in a broad manner, since jurisdictions and approval agencies vary, as do their responsibilities. Where public safety is primary, the authority having jurisdiction may be a federal, state, local, or other regional department or individual such as a fire chief; fire marshal; chief of a fire prevention bureau, labor department, or health department; building official; electrical inspector; or others having statutory authority. For insurance purposes, an insurance inspection department, rating bureau, or other insurance company representative may be the authority having jurisdiction. In many circumstances, the property owner or his or her designated agent assumes the role of the authority having jurisdiction; at government installations, the commanding officer or departmental official may be the authority having jurisdiction.

A.3.2.4 Listed. The means for identifying listed equipment may vary for each organization concerned with product evaluation; some organizations do not recognize equipment as listed unless it is also labeled. The authority having jurisdiction should utilize the system employed by the listing organization to identify a listed product.

A.3.3.21.1 Investigator's Special Tools. Examples include heavy equipment, hydrocarbon detectors, ignitible liquid detection canine teams, microscopes, flash point testers, and so forth.

A.3.3.21.2 Standard Equipment and Tools. An investigator's standard equipment and tools include a high-resolution camera, flash, and film or media; a flashlight; a shovel; a broom; hand tools; a tape measure or other measuring device; safety clothing and equipment; and evidence collection equipment and supplies. Examples of safety clothing and equipment are found in the safety chapter of NFPA 921.

A.4.1.1 Job Performance Requirements (JPRs) are organized according to duties. Duties describe major job functions and result from a job task analysis. JPRs, in total, define the tasks that investigators must be able to perform to be qualified; however, it is not logical, nor the committee's intent, that each and every JPR be performed during each investigation. Rather, the investigator should correctly apply selected JPRs as related to the investigation demands or the individual responsibilities.

A.4.1.2 The basic methodology for fire investigation involves collecting data, then developing and testing hypotheses *(see the methodology chapter of NFPA 921)*. The methodology recommended is the scientific method. Key steps in the scientific method are as follows:

(1) Recognize the need (identify the problem)
(2) Define the problem
(3) Collect data
(4) Analyze the data
(5) Develop the hypotheses (inductive reasoning)
(6) Test the hypotheses (deductive reasoning)
(7) Select final hypothesis

Developing hypotheses is an ongoing process of data collection and evaluation that happens throughout the investigation. Hypotheses are generally developed and tested for evaluating fire spread and growth, evaluating the nature of fire patterns, and determining origin, cause, and responsibility.

Testing of hypotheses can be either experimental or cognitive. Ultimately, the hypotheses and conclusions reached are only as dependable as the data used or available. Each investigator must apply a level of confidence in that opinion. For additional information regarding evaluation methods see ASTM E678, *Standard Practice for Evaluation of Scientific or Technical Data.*

A.4.1.3 For additional information concerning safety requirements or training, see applicable local, state, or federal occupational safety and health regulations and *Safety at Scenes of Fire and Related Incidents.*

A.4.1.4 Fire investigators are encouraged to interact with other professionals or organizations in their respective communities. The interaction is important for the effective transfer of information, which can be general, such as what is related in training seminars or journals, or specific to one particular incident.

A.4.1.5 It is understood that fire investigators with arrest powers, fire investigators without arrest powers, and private sector fire investigators can utilize this standard. The following is a list of those legal and regulatory requirements that are critical within the fire investigation field. It is the responsibility of the AHJ to select those issues that are pertinent to its respective agency or organization. Those selected issues should then serve as the measurement criteria or training guideline for the AHJ.

Due process issues (stated in task terms) are as follows: Conduct search and seizure, conduct arrests, conduct interviews, maintain chain of custody, utilize criminal and civil statutes applicable to the situation, and interpret and utilize contract law and insurance law. Show due process of civil rights laws, privacy laws, the fair credit reporting act, laws of trespass and invasion of privacy, laws of libel and slander, laws of punitive damages and attorney-client privilege, rules of evidence including spoliation, and other laws applicable to the AHJ.

N A.4.1.7 Up-to-date information on these topics can be found in the current edition of NFPA 921, which is written on a basic level for competency in fire and explosion investigation and updated on a three-year cycle. As stated in NFPA 921, "The purpose of the document is to establish guidelines and recommendations for the safe and systematic investigation or analysis of fire and explosion incidents." . . . "The document is designed to produce a systematic, working framework or outline by which effective fire and explosion investigation and origin and cause analysis can be accomplished." NFPA 921 also states, "[It] is not intended as a comprehensive scientific or engineering text. Although many scientific and engineering concepts are presented within the text, the user is cautioned that these concepts are presented at an elementary level and additional technical sources, training, and education may often need to be utilized in an investigation.". . ."The documents or portions thereof listed in this [document] are referenced within this guide."

A.4.2 Documents reviewed when a scene is not otherwise available can include but not be limited to incident reports, notes, photographs, diagrams and sketches, evidence, witness statements, test results, laboratory reports, and other information that would assist in the determination of the origin and cause.

△ A.4.2.2 For additional information concerning safety requirements or training, see applicable local, state, or federal occupational safety and health regulations; NFPA 470; the most current edition of IAAI *Fire Investigator Health and Safety Best Practices*; and the safety chapter of NFPA 921.

A.4.2.8 Examples of tampered systems are fire doors propped open, sprinkler systems shut down, and detection systems disabled. Examples of system failures include construction features such as compartmentation or fire doors that do not confine a fire, sprinkler systems that do not control a fire, smoke control systems that do not function correctly, HVAC systems that do not perform adequately, and alarm systems that fail to provide prompt notification. It is always important to consider the design and intention of the system. Investigators should keep in mind the possibility that systems might not have failed to function, but rather, might have been overcome by the fire development.

A.4.3.2 The use of a high-resolution camera is highly recommended. The use of various video camera systems to supplement visual documentation can be utilized and is encouraged.

N A.4.3.3 For more information and sample forms for scene documentation, see NFPA 921, Figure A.16.3.2(a) through Figure A.16.3.2(k). For sample forms for documentation of compartment fire modeling data, see NFPA 921, Figure A.16.3.2(k).

A.4.4.2 Fire investigators should determine and identify in advance what authority and specific need each may have to seize and hold item(s) considered to be evidence. Where such authority or need is lacking, items should not be seized.

For additional information regarding evidence collection methods, see ASTM E860, *Standard Practice for Examining and Preparing Items that Are or May Become Involved in Criminal or Civil Litigation*.

For additional information regarding evidence collection methods, see ASTM E1188, *Standard Practice for Collection and Preservation of Information and Physical Items by a Technical Investigator*.

A.4.6.5 For additional information regarding evaluation methods, see ASTM E678, *Standard Practice for Evaluation of Scientific or Technical Data*.

A.4.7.1 For additional information regarding the contents of a written report and evaluation methods, see ASTM E620, *Standard Practice for Reporting Opinions of Scientific or Technical Experts*, and ASTM E678, *Standard Practice for Evaluation of Scientific or Technical Data*.

△ Annex B Explanation of the Professional Qualifications Standards and Concepts of Job Performance Requirements (JPRs)

This annex is not a part of the requirements of this NFPA document but is included for informational purposes only.

△ B.1 Explanation of the Professional Qualifications Standards and Concepts of Job Performance Requirements (JPRs). The primary benefit of establishing national professional qualifications standards is to provide both public and private sectors with a framework of the job requirements for the fire service. Other benefits include enhancement of the profession, individual as well as organizational growth and development, and standardization of practices.

NFPA professional qualifications standards identify the minimum job performance requirements (JPRs) for specific emergency services levels and positions. The standards can be used for training design and evaluation, certification, measuring and critiquing on-the-job performance, defining hiring practices, job descriptions, and setting organizational policies, procedures, and goals.

Professional qualifications standards for specific jobs are organized by major areas of responsibility defined as *duties*. For example, the firefighter's duties might include fire department communications, fireground operations, and preparedness and maintenance, whereas the fire and life safety educator's duties might include education and implementation, planning and development, and evaluation. Duties are major functional areas of responsibility within a specific job.

The professional qualifications standards are written as JPRs. JPRs describe the performance required for a specific job and are grouped according to the duties of the job. The complete list of JPRs for each duty defines what an individual must be able to do in order to perform and achieve that duty.

B.2 The Parts of a JPR.

B.2.1 Critical Components. The JPR comprises three critical components, which are as follows:

(1) Task to be performed, partial description using an action verb (*See Figure B.2.1 for examples of action verbs used in the creation of JPRs.*)
(2) Tools, equipment, or materials that are to be provided to complete the task
(3) Evaluation parameters and performance outcomes

Table B.2.1 gives an example of the critical components of a JPR.

B.2.1.1 The Task to Be Performed. The first component is a concise statement of what the individual is required to do. A significant aspect of that phrase is the use of an action verb, which sets the expectation for what is to be accomplished.

B.2.1.2 Tools, Equipment, or Materials that Should Be Provided for Successful Completion of the Task. This component

Table B.2.1 Component Example

(1) Task to be performed	(1) Perform overhaul at a fire scene,
(2) Tools, equipment, or materials	(2) given PPE, an attack line, hand tools, flashlight, and an assignment,
(3) Evaluation parameters and performance outcomes	(3) so that structural integrity is not compromised, all hidden fires are discovered, fire cause evidence is preserved, and the fire is extinguished.

ensures that all the individuals completing the task are given the same tools, equipment, or materials when they are being evaluated. Both the individual and the evaluator will know what should be provided in order for the individual to complete the task.

△ **B.2.1.3 Evaluation Parameters and Performance Outcomes.** This component defines for both the performer and the evaluator how well the individual should perform each task. The JPR guides performance toward successful completion by identifying evaluation parameters and performance outcomes. This portion of the JPR promotes consistency in evaluation by reducing the variables used to gauge performance.

N **B.2.2 Requisite Knowledge and Skills.** In addition to these three components, a JPR describes requisite knowledge and skills. As the term *requisite* suggests, these are the necessary knowledge and skills the individual should have prior to being able to perform the task. Requisite knowledge and skills are the foundation for task performance.

N **B.2.3 Examples.** With the components and requisites combined, a JPR might be similar to the two examples in B.2.3.1 and B.2.3.2.

B.2.3.1 Example: Firefighter I. Perform overhaul at a fire scene, given PPE, attack line, hand tools, flashlight, and an assignment, so that structural integrity is not compromised, all hidden fires are discovered, fire cause evidence is preserved, and the fire is extinguished.

(A) Requisite Knowledge. Knowledge of types of fire attack lines and water application devices for overhaul, water application methods for extinguishment that limit water damage, types of tools and methods used to expose hidden fire, dangers associated with overhaul, signs of area of origin or signs of arson, and reasons for protection of fire scene.

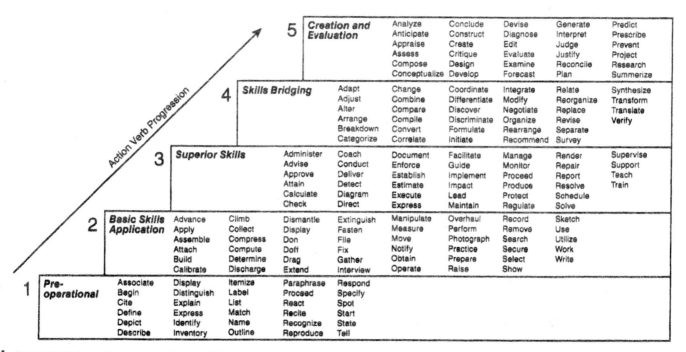

N **FIGURE B.2.1 Examples of Action Verbs.**

(B) Requisite Skills. The ability to deploy and operate an attack line; remove flooring, ceiling, and wall components to expose void spaces without compromising structural integrity; apply water for maximum effectiveness; expose and extinguish hidden fires in walls, ceilings, and subfloor spaces; recognize and preserve signs of area of origin and arson; and evaluate for complete extinguishment.

B.2.3.2 Example: Fire and Life Safety Educator II. Prepare a written budget proposal for a specific program or activity, given budgetary guidelines, program needs, and delivery expense projections, so that all guidelines are followed and the budget identifies all the program needs.

(A) Requisite Knowledge. Knowledge of budgetary process; governmental accounting procedures; federal, tribal, state, and local laws; organizational bidding process; and organization purchase requests.

(B) Requisite Skills. The ability to estimate project costs; complete budget forms; requisition/purchase orders; collect, organize, and format budgetary information; complete program budget proposal; and complete purchase requests.

△ **B.3 Potential Uses of JPRs.**

△ **B.3.1 Certification.** JPRs can be used to establish the evaluation criteria for certification at a specific job level. When used for certification, evaluation should be based on the successful completion of the JPRs.

The evaluator should verify the attainment of requisite knowledge and skills prior to JPRs evaluation. Verification could be through documentation review or testing.

The individual seeking certification should be evaluated on the completion of the JPRs. The individual should perform the task and be evaluated based on the evaluation parameters and/or performance outcomes. This performance-based evaluation is based on practical exercises for psychomotor skills and written examinations for cognitive skills.

Psychomotor skills are those physical skills that can be demonstrated or observed. Cognitive skills cannot be observed but rather are evaluated on how an individual completes a task (process-oriented) or on a task's outcome (product-oriented).

Performance evaluation requires that individuals be given the tools, equipment, or materials listed in the JPR in order to complete the task.

Table B.3.1 provides examples of how assessment methodologies can be utilized by a certifying body.

△ **B.3.2 Curriculum Development and Training Design and Evaluation.** The statements contained in this document that refer to job performance were designed and written as JPRs. Although a resemblance to instructional objectives might be present, these statements should not be used in a teaching situation until after they have been modified for instructional use.

JPRs state the behaviors required to perform specific skills on the job, as opposed to a learning situation. These statements should be converted into instructional objectives with behaviors, conditions, and the degree to be measured within the educational environment.

While the differences between JPRs and instructional objectives are subtle in appearance, their purposes differ. JPRs state what is necessary to perform the job in practical and actual experience. Instructional objectives, on the other hand, are used to identify what students should do at the end of a training session and are stated in behavioral terms that are measurable in the training environment.

By converting JPRs into instructional objectives, instructors would be able to clarify performance expectations and avoid confusion caused by the use of statements designed for purposes other than teaching. Instructors would also be able to add jurisdictional elements of performance into the learning objectives as intended by the developers.

Requisite skills and knowledge could be converted into enabling objectives, which would help to define the course content. The course content would include each item of the requisite knowledge and skills, ensuring that the course content supports the terminal objective.

N **B.3.2.1 Example: Converting a Firefighter I JPR into an Instructional Objective.** The instructional objectives are just two of several instructional objectives that would be written to support the terminal objective based on the JPR.

JPR: Perform overhaul at a fire scene, given PPE, attack line, hand tools, flashlight, and an assignment, so that structural integrity is not compromised, all hidden fires are discovered, fire cause evidence is preserved, and the fire is extinguished.

Instructional Objective (Cognitive): The Firefighter I will identify and describe five safety considerations associated with structural integrity compromise during overhaul as part of a written examination.

Instructional Objective (Psychomotor): The Firefighter I will demonstrate the designed use of tools and equipment during overhaul to locate and extinguish hidden fires without compromising structural integrity.

N **B.3.2.2 Example: Converting a Fire and Life Safety Educator II JPR into an Instructional Objective.** This instructional objective is just one of several instructional objectives that could be written to support the terminal objective based on the JPR.

JPR: Prepare a written budget proposal for a specific program or activity, given budgetary guidelines, program needs, and delivery expense projections, so that all guidelines are followed and the budget identifies all program needs.

Instructional Objective (Cognitive): The Fire and Life Safety Educator II will list and describe the bidding process for the purchase of a published program using budgetary guidelines, program needs, and the guidelines established by local organizational procedures as part of a written examination.

Instructional Objective (Psychomotor): The Fire and Life Safety Educator II will lead in the purchase of a specific fire and life safety educational program by following the bidding process to completion, using local organizational guidelines, including budgetary procedures, program needs, and delivery expense projections.

Table B.3.1 Assessment Methodology Sample Utilization

Assessment of...	How Assessed?	How Scored?	Methodology is Likely...
Knowledge/facts *Action verb examples:* identify, define, list, cite, state, choose, name	A written test in which the candidate is required to provide specific answers to specific questions related to the JPRs *Examples:* multiple choice, sequencing, true/false, fill-in-the-blank	Responses are scored in relation to the answer that has been determined to be correct.	Cognitive
A manipulative skill in real time *Action verb examples:* climb, build, perform, raise, haul, don	A skills test to evaluate a candidate's ability to perform physical tasks in real time *Examples:* donning SCBA, raising ladders, tying rescue knots	The directly observed performance with the correct performance outcome of the skill is normally indicated as part of the yes/no or pass/fail scoring checklist.	Psychomotor (skills)
A cognitive skill that cannot be directly observed; the application of knowledge to yield a product *Action verb examples:* develop, create, write	A work product created by the candidate usually outside of the classroom setting *Examples:* creating a budget, report, proposal, lesson plan, incident action plan	Scoring rubric for expected responses evaluating how a candidate completes the task outcome after submission. Used to differentiate consistently between different degrees of candidate performance.	Product
A mental activity to perform a cognitive skill in real time that cannot be directly observed *Action verb examples:* inspect, investigate	Candidate performs the activity in the presence of the evaluator; the verbalization of mental thought "First, I..., then I...," etc. *Examples:* performing an inspection, conducting an investigation	Scoring rubric with questions and expected verbal responses. Used to differentiate consistently between different degrees of candidate performance.	Process
Documentation of the candidate's experience, training, and education against all JPRs *Action verb examples:* attend, participate, testify	A list of acceptable documents or items for each and every JPR *Examples:* coursework at training or college, participation in a certain number of investigations, testifying at court	*This portfolio is evaluated using* criteria that have been identified by the agency.	*Portfolio*

B.4 Other Uses of JPRs. While the professional qualifications standards are used to establish minimum JPRs for qualification, they have been recognized as guides for the development of training and certification programs, as well as a number of other potential uses.

These areas might include the following:

(1) *Employee Evaluation/Performance Critiquing.* The professional qualifications standards can be used as a guide by both the supervisor and the employee during an evaluation. The JPRs for a specific job define tasks that are essential to perform on the job as well as the evaluation criteria to measure completion of the tasks.

(2) *Establishing Hiring Criteria.* The professional qualifications standards can be helpful in a number of ways to further the establishment of hiring criteria. The authority having jurisdiction (AHJ) could simply require certification at a specific job level — for example, Firefighter I. The JPRs could also be used as the basis for pre-employment screening to establish essential minimal tasks and the related evaluation criteria. An added benefit is that individuals interested in employment can work toward the minimal hiring criteria at local colleges.

(3) *Employee Development.* The professional qualifications standards can be practical for both the employee and the employer in developing a plan for the employee's growth within the organization. The JPRs and the associated requisite knowledge and skills can be used as a guide to determine the additional training and education required for the employee to master the job or profession.

(4) *Succession Planning.* Succession planning addresses the efficient placement of individuals into jobs in response to current needs and anticipated future needs. A career development path can be established for targeted employees to prepare them for growth within the organization. The JPRs and requisite knowledge and skills could then be used to develop an educational path to aid in the

employee's advancement within the organization or profession.

(5) *Establishing Organizational Policies, Procedures, and Goals.* The professional qualifications standards can be functional for incorporating policies, procedures, and goals into the organization or agency.

N B.5 Bibliography.

Annett, J., and N. E. Stanton, *Task Analysis.* London and New York: Taylor and Francis, 2000.

Brannick, M. T., and E. L. Levine, *Job Analysis: Methods, Research, and Applications for Human Resource Management in the New Millennium.* Thousand Oaks, CA: Sage Publications, 2002.

Dubois, D. D., *Competency-Based Performance Improvement: A Strategy for Organizational Change.* Amherst, MA: HRD Press, 1999.

Fine, S. A., and S. F. Cronshaw, *Functional Job Analysis: A Foundation for Human Resources Management* (Applied Psychology Series). Mahwah, NJ: Lawrence Erlbaum Associates, 1999.

Gupta, K., C. M. Sleezer (editor), and D. F. Russ-Eft (editor), *A Practical Guide to Needs Assessment.* San Francisco: Jossey-Bass/Pfeiffer, 2007.

Hartley, D. E., *Job Analysis at the Speed of Reality.* Amherst, MA: HRD Press, 1999.

Hodell, C., *ISD from the Ground Up: A No-Nonsense Approach to Instructional Design,* 3rd edition. Alexandria, VA: American Society for Training & Development, 2011.

Jonassen, D. H., M. Tessmer, and W. H. Hannum, *Task Analysis Methods for Instructional Design.* Mahwah, NJ: Lawrence Erlbaum Associates, 1999.

McArdle, G., *Conducting a Needs Analysis (Fifty-Minute Book).* Boston: Crisp Learning, 1998.

McCain, D. V., *Creating Training Courses (When You're Not a Trainer).* Alexandria, VA: American Society for Training & Development, 1999.

NFPA 1001, *Standard for Fire Fighter Professional Qualifications,* 2019 edition.

NFPA 1035, *Standard on Fire and Life Safety Educator, Public Information Officer, Youth Firesetter Intervention Specialist, and Youth Firesetter Program Manager Professional Qualifications,* 2015 edition.

Phillips, J. J., *In Action: Performance Analysis and Consulting.* Alexandria, VA: American Society for Training & Development, 2000.

Phillips, J. J., and E. F. Holton III, *In Action: Conducting Needs Assessment.* Alexandria, VA: American Society for Training & Development, 1995.

Robinson, D. G., and J. C. Robinson (editors), *Moving from Training to Performance: A Practical Guidebook.* Alexandria, VA: American Society for Training & Development; San Francisco: Berrett-Koehler, 1998.

Schippmann, J. S., *Strategic Job Modeling: Working at the Core of Integrated Human Resources.* Mahwah, NJ: Lawrence Erlbaum Associates, 1999.

Shepherd, A., *Hierarchical Task Analysis.* London and New York: Taylor and Francis, 2000.

Zemke, R., and T. Kramlinger, *Figuring Things Out: A Trainer's Guide to Needs and Task Analysis.* New York: Perseus Books, 1993.

N   Annex C   An Overview of JPRs for Fire Investigator

This annex is not a part of the requirements of this NFPA document but is included for informational purposes only.

N C.1 Fire Investigators. The matrices shown in Table C.1 are included to provide the user of the standard with an overview of the JPRs for fire investigators and the progression of the various levels found in the document. They are intended to assist the user of the document with the implementation of the requirements and the development of training programs using the JPRs.

Table C.1 Fire Investigator

Fire Investigator	
4.2 Scene Examination.	
Duties shall include inspecting, evaluating, and analyzing the fire scene or evidence of the scene, and conducting a comprehensive review of documentation generated during the examination(s) of the scene if the scene is no longer available, so as to determine the area or point of origin, source of ignition, material(s) ignited, and action or activity that brought the ignition source and materials together and to assess the subsequent progression, extinguishment, and containment of the fire.	
4.2.2	Conduct an exterior survey, given standard equipment and tools, so that evidence is identified and preserved, fire damage is interpreted and analyzed, hazards are identified to avoid injuries, accessibility to the property is determined, and all potential means of ingress and egress are discovered.
4.2.3	Conduct an interior survey, given standard equipment and tools, so that areas of potential evidentiary value requiring further examination are identified and preserved, the evidentiary value of contents is determined, and hazards are identified in order to avoid injuries.
4.2.4	Interpret and analyze fire patterns, given standard equipment and tools and some structural or content remains, so that each pattern is identified and analyzed with respect to the burning characteristics of the material involved, the stage of fire development, the effects of ventilation within the context of the scene, the relationship with all patterns observed, and the understanding of the methods of heat transfer that led to the formation of the patterns identified and analyzed, and the sequence in which the patterns were produced is determined.
4.2.5	Interpret and analyze fire patterns, given standard equipment and tools and some structural or content remains, so that fire development, fire spread, and the sequence in which fire patterns were developed (i.e., sequential pattern analysis) are determined; methods and effects of suppression are analyzed; fire patterns and effects indicating a hypothetical area or areas of origin are recognized and tested; false or refuted hypothetical areas of origin are eliminated; and all fire patterns are tested against the data, such that the area(s) of origin is correctly identified.
4.2.6	Examine and remove fire debris, given standard or, if necessary, special equipment and tools, so that fire patterns and fire effects concealed by debris are discovered and analyzed; all debris within the potential area(s) of origin is checked for fire cause evidence; potential ignition source(s) is identified; and evidence is preserved without investigator-inflicted damage or contamination.
4.2.7	Reconstruct potential area(s) of origin, given standard and, if needed, special equipment and tools as well as sufficient personnel, so that all protected areas and fire patterns are identified and correlated to contents or structural remains; and items potentially critical to cause determination are returned to their prefire location as a means of hypothesis testing, such that the area(s) or point(s) of origin is discovered.
4.2.8	Inspect and analyze the performance of building systems, including fire protection, detection and suppression systems, HVAC, electricity and electrical systems, fuel gas systems, and building compartmentation, given standard and special equipment and tools, so that a determination can be made as to the need for expert resources; an operating system's impact on fire growth and spread is considered in identifying origin areas; defeated and failed systems are identified; and the system's potential as a fire cause is recognized.
4.2.9	Discriminate the effects of explosions from other types of damage, given standard equipment and tools, so that an explosion is identified and its evidence is preserved.
4.3 Documenting the Scene.	
4.3.1	Diagram the scene, given standard tools and equipment, so that the scene is accurately represented and evidence, pertinent contents, significant patterns, and area(s) or point(s) of origin are identified.
4.3.2	Photographically document the scene, given standard tools and equipment, so that the scene is accurately depicted and the photographs support scene findings.
4.3.3	Construct investigative notes, given a fire scene, available documents (e.g., prefire plans and inspection reports), and interview information, so that the notes are accurate, provide further documentation of the scene, and represent complete documentation of the scene findings.
4.4 Evidence Collection/Preservation.	
4.4.1	Utilize proper procedures for managing victims and fatalities, given a protocol and appropriate personnel, so that all evidence is discovered and preserved and the protocol procedures are followed.

(continues)

N Table C.1   *Continued*

	Fire Investigator
4.4.2	Locate, document, collect, label, package, and store evidence, given standard or special tools and equipment and evidence collection materials, so that evidence is properly identified, preserved, collected, packaged, and stored for use in testing, legal, or other proceedings and examinations; ensuring cross-contamination and investigator-inflicted damage to evidentiary items are avoided; and the chain of custody is established.
4.4.3	Select evidence for analysis, given all information from the investigation, so that items for analysis support specific investigation needs.
4.4.4	Maintain a chain of custody, given standard investigative tools, marking tools, and evidence tags or logs, so that written documentation exists for each piece of evidence and evidence is secured.
4.4.5	Dispose of evidence, given jurisdictional or agency regulations and file information, so that the disposal is timely, safely conducted, and in compliance with jurisdictional or agency requirements.
	4.5 Interview.
4.5.1	Develop an interview plan, given no special tools or equipment, so that the plan reflects a strategy to further determine the fire cause and affix responsibility and includes a relevant questioning strategy for each individual to be interviewed that promotes the efficient use of the investigator's time.
4.5.2	Conduct interviews, given incident information, so that pertinent information is obtained, follow-up questions are asked, responses to all questions are elicited, and the response to each question is documented accurately.
4.5.3	Evaluate interview information, given interview transcripts or notes and incident data, so that all interview data is individually analyzed and correlated with all other interviews, corroborative and conflictive information is documented, and new leads are developed.
	4.6 Post-Incident Investigation.
4.6.1	Gather reports and records, given no special tools, equipment, or materials, so that all gathered documents are applicable to the investigation, complete, and authentic; the chain of custody is maintained; and the material is admissible in a legal proceeding.
4.6.2	Evaluate the investigative file, given all available file information, so that areas for further investigation are identified, the relationship between gathered documents and information is interpreted, and corroborative evidence and information discrepancies are discovered.
4.6.3	Coordinate expert resources, given the investigative file, reports, and documents, so that the expert's competencies are matched to the specific investigation needs, financial expenditures are justified, and utilization clearly furthers the investigative goals of determining cause or affixing responsibility.
4.6.4	Establish evidence as to motive and/or opportunity, given an incendiary fire, so that the evidence is supported by documentation and meets the evidentiary requirements of the jurisdiction.
4.6.5	Formulate an opinion concerning origin, cause, or responsibility for the fire, given all investigative findings, so that the opinion regarding origin, cause, or responsibility for a fire is supported by the data, facts, records, reports, documents, scientific references, and evidence.
	4.7 Presentations.
4.7.1	Prepare a written report, given investigative findings, so that the report accurately reflects the facts, data, and scientific principles on which the investigator relied; clearly identifies and expresses the investigator's opinions and conclusions; and contains the reasoning by which each opinion or conclusion was reached in order to meet the requirements of the intended audience(s).
4.7.2	Express investigative findings verbally, given investigative findings, notes, a time allotment, and a specific audience, so that the information is accurate, the presentation is completed within the allotted time, and the presentation includes only need-to-know information for the intended audience.
4.7.3	Testify during legal proceedings, given investigative findings, so that the testimony accurately reflects the facts, data, and scientific principles on which the investigator relied; clearly identifies and expresses the investigator's opinions and conclusions; and contains the reasoning by which each opinion or conclusion was reached.

Annex D Terms and Concepts

This annex is not a part of the requirements of this NFPA document but is included for informational purposes only.

D.1 General. This annex provides examples of concepts and terms for evaluating "requisite knowledge" prior to job performance requirement (JPR) evaluation. The fire investigator should have a basic understanding of the terms and concepts in the examples in D.1.1 through D.1.4 in order to successfully complete the tasks listed in the JPRs.

D.1.1 The term *fire science* as used in this standard refers to a group of interrelated subjects listed in D.1.1(1) through D.1.1(4).

(1) *Fire chemistry:*

    (a) States of matter (gases, liquids, and solids)
    (b) Chemical reactions (fire triangle and fire tetrahedron)
    (c) Stoichiometry
    (d) Chemical composition of common combustibles
    (e) Phase changes and reactions that might require or produce energy (exothermic and endothermic processes)
    (f) Material properties (density, conductivity, specific heat, deformation, melting, vaporization, vapor pressure)
    (g) Structural properties (effect of temperatures on properties)
    (h) Combustion properties (flammable limits, minimum ignition energy, critical flux for ignition, ignition temperatures, heat of combustion, flash point of liquid, and fire point)
    (i) Fuels
    (j) Complete and incomplete combustion reaction products (combustion efficiency and role of fuel/air ratio in product composition)
    (k) The response of materials to heat (melting, dehydration, pyrolysis, charring, loss of mass, deformation, evaporation, and calcination)
    (l) Different temperature scales

(2) *Thermodynamics:*

    (a) Definition of energy, work, and power
    (b) Ideal gas law ($PV = nRT$)
    (c) Conservation of energy
    (d) Phase changes and energy requirements
    (e) Vapor pressures
    (f) Heat capacity

(3) *Fire dynamics: Concepts and units of energy, heat release rate (HRR) (power), and heat flux:*

    (a) Means by which temperature can be measured
    (b) Incorporation of temperature measurement controls in devices and appliances
    (c) Piloted and spontaneous ignition of solids
    (d) Smoldering and pyrolysis
    (e) Self-heating
    (f) Heat transfer (definition, units, conduction, convection, and radiation)
    (g) Thermal inertia, thermal conductivity, density, and specific heat (thermally thin and thermally thick)
    (h) Natural versus forced convection
    (i) Point source radiant heat transfer
    (j) Flame spread (counter- and concurrent-flow)
    (k) Orientation of fuels and the effect on flame spread

    (l) Flames (height, tilt, temperatures, velocity, widths, and relationship between HRR and height)
    (m) Buoyancy
    (n) Diffusion and premixed flames
    (o) Laminar and turbulent flames
    (p) Fuel packages and associated HRRs
    (q) Fluid flows [plume development, ceiling jets (depth, temperature, and velocity), vent flows, and stack/chimney effect]
    (r) Development of a compartment fire(s)
    (s) Plumes and hot gas layer development
    (t) Vent flows (flow paths, unidirectional and bidirectional flows, exhaust and inlet flows, and neutral planes)
    (u) Flashover (definition, recognition, and impact on damage)
    (v) Full-room involvement (definition, impact on damage, and how to interpret as a fire investigator)
    (w) Relationship of compartment fire dynamics phenomena to fire pattern development (plume-generated patterns, hot gas layer–generated patterns, ventilation-generated patterns, and effects of full-room involvement)
    (x) Suppression effects (influence on damage and on spread)
    (y) Ventilation-limited burning
    (z) Effects of fuel location in a compartment

(4) *Explosion dynamics:*

    (a) How chemistry, physics, fire science, engineering disciplines of fluid and solid mechanics, and heat transfer interact to influence explosion behavior
    (b) Deflagration versus detonation
    (c) Chemical, mechanical, BLEVE, electrical, and dust explosions
    (d) Recognition of damage caused by fuel/air explosions
    (e) Recognition of damage caused by low explosives
    (f) Recognition of damage caused by high explosives
    (g) Positive and negative pressure waves
    (h) Cascading explosions
    (i) Flame front and pressure propagation in a flammable gas cloud

N D.1.1.1 Information regarding the subjects in D.1.1 is summarized in the appropriate chapters of NFPA 921 as follows:

(1) *Fire chemistry* — NFPA 921, Chapter 5, Basic Fire Science
(2) *Fire dynamics* — NFPA 921, Chapter 5, Basic Fire Science; Chapter 6, Fire Patterns; and Chapter 22, Failure Analysis and Analytical Tools
(3) *Explosion dynamics* — NFPA 921, Chapter 23, Explosions

N D.1.2 Fire Investigation. The term *fire investigation* as used in this standard refers to a group of interrelated subjects listed in D.1.2(1) through D.1.2(5):

(1) *Fire analysis:*

    (a) How to determine the origin of a fire
    (b) How to determine the cause of a fire
    (c) How to determine the responsibility for the fire
    (d) How to conduct a failure analysis to understand the cause
    (e) How other disciplines such as chemistry, engineering, or law enforcement can be integrated into a fire analysis

(2) *Fire investigation methodology:*

  (a) Legal contexts in which fire investigations are conducted

  (b) The importance of using a systematic process when conducting fire investigations

  (c) The scientific method and its application for fire investigation

  (d) Logical reasoning and faulty reasoning

  (e) Appropriate application of the process of elimination

  (f) "Negative corpus methodology"

  (g) Methods for data collection, data analysis, hypothesis formation, and hypothesis testing

  (h) How to correctly employ the steps of the scientific method

  (i) How to identify and manage bias

  (j) Understand bias: confirmation bias, expectation bias

  (k) How to demonstrate adherence to the scientific method

  (l) Interviewing techniques

  (m) Scene processing methods

  (n) The impact of *Daubert v. Merrill Dow Pharmaceuticals* U.S. 579 (1993) and other applicable admissibility standards

(3) *Fire investigation technology:* The investigator should recognize that there are tools available for various tasks (e.g., tablets, 3D laser scanning, X-ray, unmanned aircraft system (UAS), computer modeling, time lines, and shovels)

(4) *Evidence documentation, collection, preservation, and disposition. (Rules of evidence):*

  (a) The concept of spoliation, how to avoid spoliation, and potential sanctions

  (b) Recognize when it might be necessary to suspend activities on the fire scene so that interested parties can be notified

  (c) How to identify evidence

  (d) How to avoid cross-contamination

  (e) Documentation of evidence (photographs, diagrams, measurements, evidence log, and labeling)

  (f) How to collect, protect, preserve, package, store, and dispose of evidence

  (g) How to complete and preserve the chain of custody

(5) *Failure analysis and analytical tools:*

  (a) How to prepare a time line

  (b) Different kinds of fire models (hand calculations, zone models, and field models)

  (c) Data required for input in each kind of model (structural dimensions, lining materials, fuels, ventilation, fire protection elements, and changes during the fire)

  (d) Type of output that the various models can provide

  (e) Limitations and uncertainty involved in modeling

  (f) Uses of the various analytical tools available

N **D.1.2.1** Information regarding the subjects in D.1.2 is summarized in the following resources:

(1) *Fire investigation methodology* — NFPA 921, Chapter 4, Basic Methodology; Chapter 12, Legal Considerations; Chapter 18, Origin Determination; and Chapter 19, Fire Cause Determination.

(2) *Evidence* — NFPA 921, Chapter 12, Legal Considerations; Chapter 16, Documentation of the Investigation; and Chapter 17, Physical Evidence. ASTM Standards E860, E1188, E1459, and E1492 define requirements for evidence topics.

(3) *Failure analysis and analytical tools* — NFPA 921, Chapter 22, Failure Analysis and Analytical Tools.

N **D.1.3 Fire Scene Safety.** The term *fire safety* as used in this standard refers to a group of interrelated subjects listed in D.1.3(1) through D.1.3(3).

(1) *Hazard recognition, evaluation, and mitigation:*

  (a) How to conduct a site safety assessment

  (b) Recognition and evaluation of hazards (structural, mechanical, electrical, chemical, biological, confined space, and physical)

  (c) The procedures to mitigate hazards

  (d) Lockout/tagout

  (e) Recognition of incident command system (ICS)

  (f) Assignment of a safety officer

  (g) Selection, donning and doffing, and maintenance of PPE

  (h) Proper decontamination

(2) *Hazardous materials:*

  (a) How to evaluate safety data sheets (SDS)

  (b) How to select proper PPE, given the hazardous material identified

  (c) The level of training required to operate in a hazardous environment

  (d) Decontamination procedures

  (e) Placard systems *[For NFPA and globally harmonized systems (GHS), see NFPA 704.]*

  (f) Collection, transportation (DOT), storage, and disposal of hazardous evidence

  (g) EPA and other jurisdictional regulations related to disposal

(3) *Safety regulations:*

  (a) Jurisdictional safety requirements

  (b) Transportation of hazardous evidence

  (c) Jurisdictional environmental regulations

N **D.1.3.1** Information regarding the subjects in D.1.3 can be found in the following resources:

(1) *Hazard recognition* — NFPA 921, Chapter 13, Safety.

(2) *Hazardous materials* — NFPA 921, Chapter 13, Safety. NFPA 400 contains requirements regarding hazardous materials. Operating around hazardous material is often covered by state and federal laws, which must be understood by investigators working in different jurisdictions. Knowledge and skills in this area are taught in professional training courses and seminars provided by a variety of sources.

(3) *Safety regulations* — NFPA 921, Chapter 13, Safety; 29 CFR 1910; and 29 CFR 1926. This information is taught in professional training courses and seminars provided by a variety of sources.

N **D.1.4 Building Systems.** The term *building systems* as used in this standard refers to a group of interrelated subjects listed in D.1.4(1) through D.1.4(4):

(1) *Types of construction:*

  (a) Recognizing different classifications of building construction

(b) How the features of the building will influence fire growth and spread

(2) *Fire protection systems:*

(a) Passive and active fire protection and how they influence fire dynamics

(b) How to recognize and collect the data available from fire protection systems

(c) How to avoid spoliation in examining and documenting the systems and prevent the loss of volatile data

(d) The differences between initiating and notification devices

(e) Smoke management systems

(f) How to document the systems and their activation

(g) How to identify when such systems perform or fail to perform their intended functions

(h) In cases of failures, knowledge of what steps to take to understand the cause of the failure or reach out to a subject matter expert

(i) Note: Examination, analysis, and documentation of fire protection systems could require the assistance of a fire protection professional.

(3) *Electricity and electrical systems:*

(a) The design, function, and components of residential electrical systems

(b) How to determine whether the electrical system was energized at the time of the fire

(c) How to determine whether the electrical system played a part in the initiation or spread of a fire, which includes the ability to distinguish electrical damage from environmental damage

(d) The ability to decide when it is necessary to call in someone with more advanced electrical knowledge

(e) How to conduct and interpret an arc survey

(f) How to describe and identify how electrical energy can cause heating, which can be the ignition source of the fire (e.g., high-resistance heating, arcing through char, and overloading)

(4) *Fuel gas systems:*

(a) The design and components of a gas system

(b) The differences between propane gas and natural gas

(c) How to document the gas source and its distribution to the appliances

(d) How to document the combustion air supply and flue gas exhaust

(e) The operation of residential gas appliances

(f) The distribution system of gas to the structure

(g) How to determine the source of the fugitive fuel gas

▼ D.1.4.1 Information regarding the subjects in D.1.4 can be found in the following resources:

(1) *Types of construction* — NFPA 921 and NFPA 220.

(2) *Fire protection systems* — NFPA 921, Chapter 8, Active Fire Protection Systems.

(3) *Electricity and electrical systems* — NFPA 921, Chapter 9, Electricity and Fire, and Chapter 18, Origin and Determination. This information is taught in community college courses and in electrician apprenticeships.

Annex E Informational References

E.1 Referenced Publications. The documents or portions thereof listed in this annex are referenced within the informational sections of this standard and are not part of the requirements of this document unless also listed in Chapter 2 for other reasons.

△ **E.1.1 NFPA Publications.** National Fire Protection Association, 1 Batterymarch Park, Quincy, MA 02169-7471.

NFPA 220, *Standard on Types of Building Construction*, 2021 edition.

NFPA 400, *Hazardous Materials Code*, 2022 edition.

NFPA 470, *Hazardous Materials Standards for Responders*, 2022 edition.

NFPA 704, *Standard System for the Identification of the Hazards of Materials for Emergency Response*, 2022 edition.

NFPA 921, *Guide for Fire and Explosion Investigations*, 2021 edition.

NFPA 1001, *Standard for Fire Fighter Professional Qualifications*, 2019 edition.

NFPA 1035, *Standard on Fire and Life Safety Educator, Public Information Officer, Youth Firesetter Intervention Specialist, and Youth Firesetter Program Manager Professional Qualifications*, 2015 edition.

E.1.2 Other Publications.

E.1.2.1 ASTM Publications. ASTM International, 100 Barr Harbor Drive, P.O. Box C700, West Conshohocken, PA 19428-2959.

ASTM E620, *Standard Practice for Reporting Opinions of Scientific or Technical Experts*, 2018.

ASTM E678, *Standard Practice for Evaluation of Scientific or Technical Data*, 2013.

ASTM E860, *Standard Practice for Examining and Preparing Items That Are or May Become Involved in Criminal or Civil Litigation*, 2013e2.

ASTM E1188, *Standard Practice for Collection and Preservation of Information and Physical Items by a Technical Investigator*, 2015.

ASTM E1459, *Standard Guide for Physical Evidence Labeling and Related Documentation*, 2013.

ASTM E1492, *Standard Practice for Receiving, Documenting, Storing, and Retrieving Evidence in a Forensic Science Laboratory*, 2011 (2017).

E.1.2.2 IAAI Publications. International Association of Arson Investigators, 16901 Melford Boulevard, Suite 101 Bowie, MD 20715.

Fire Investigator Health and Safety Best Practices, May 4, 2020.

N **E.1.2.3 US Government Publications.** US Government Publishing Office, 732 North Capitol Street, NW, Washington, DC 20401-0001.

Title 29, Code of Federal Regulations, Part 1910, *Occupational Safety and Health Standards*.

Title 29, Code of Federal Regulations, Part 1926, *Safety and Health Regulations for Construction.*

N E.1.2.4 Other Publications.

Annett, J., and N. E. Stanton, *Task Analysis.* London and New York: Taylor and Francis, 2000.

Brannick, M. T., and E. L. Levine, *Job Analysis: Methods, Research, and Applications for Human Resource Management in the New Millennium.* Thousand Oaks, CA: Sage Publications, 2002.

Dubois, D. D., *Competency-Based Performance Improvement: A Strategy for Organizational Change.* Amherst, MA: HRD Press, 1999.

Fine, S. A., and S. F. Cronshaw, *Functional Job Analysis: A Foundation for Human Resources Management* (Applied Psychology Series). Mahwah, NJ: Lawrence Erlbaum Associates, 1999.

Gupta, K., C. M. Sleezer (editor), and D. F. Russ-Eft (editor), *A Practical Guide to Needs Assessment.* San Francisco: Jossey-Bass/Pfeiffer, 2007.

Hartley, D. E., *Job Analysis at the Speed of Reality.* Amherst, MA: HRD Press, 1999.

Hodell, C., *ISD from the Ground Up: A No-Nonsense Approach to Instructional Design,* 3rd edition. Alexandria, VA: American Society for Training & Development, 2011.

Jonassen, D. H., M. Tessmer, and W. H. Hannum, *Task Analysis Methods for Instructional Design.* Mahwah, NJ: Lawrence Erlbaum Associates, 1999.

McArdle, G., *Conducting a Needs Analysis (Fifty-Minute Book).* Boston: Crisp Learning, 1998.

McCain, D. V., *Creating Training Courses (When You're Not a Trainer).* Alexandria, VA: American Society for Training & Development, 1999.

Munday, J. W., *Safety at Scenes of Fire and Related Incidents.* London: Fire Protection Association, 1994.

Phillips, J. J., *In Action: Performance Analysis and Consulting.* Alexandria, VA: American Society for Training & Development, 2000.

Phillips, J. J., and E. F. Holton III, *In Action: Conducting Needs Assessment.* Alexandria, VA: American Society for Training & Development, 1995.

Robinson, D. G., and J. C. Robinson (Eds.), *Moving from Training to Performance: A Practical Guidebook.* Alexandria, VA: American Society for Training & Development; San Francisco: Berrett-Koehler, 1998.

Schippmann, J. S., *Strategic Job Modeling: Working at the Core of Integrated Human Resources.* Mahwah, NJ: Lawrence Erlbaum Associates, 1999.

Shepherd, A., *Hierarchical Task Analysis.* London and New York: Taylor and Francis, 2000.

Zemke, R., and T. Kramlinger, *Figuring Things Out: A Trainer's Guide to Needs and Task Analysis.* New York: Perseus Books, 1993.

△ E.2 Informational References. (Reserved)

E.3 References for Extracts in Informational Sections. (Reserved)

Index

Sequence of Events for the Standards Development Process

Once the current edition is published, a Standard is opened for Public Input.

Step 1 – Input Stage

- Input accepted from the public or other committees for consideration to develop the First Draft
- Technical Committee holds First Draft Meeting to revise Standard (23 weeks); Technical Committee(s) with Correlating Committee (10 weeks)
- Technical Committee ballots on First Draft (12 weeks); Technical Committee(s) with Correlating Committee (11 weeks)
- Correlating Committee First Draft Meeting (9 weeks)
- Correlating Committee ballots on First Draft (5 weeks)
- First Draft Report posted on the document information page

Step 2 – Comment Stage

- Public Comments accepted on First Draft (10 weeks) following posting of First Draft Report
- If Standard does not receive Public Comments and the Technical Committee chooses not to hold a Second Draft meeting, the Standard becomes a Consent Standard and is sent directly to the Standards Council for issuance (see Step 4) or
- Technical Committee holds Second Draft Meeting (21 weeks); Technical Committee(s) with Correlating Committee (7 weeks)
- Technical Committee ballots on Second Draft (11 weeks); Technical Committee(s) with Correlating Committee (10 weeks)
- Correlating Committee Second Draft Meeting (9 weeks)
- Correlating Committee ballots on Second Draft (8 weeks)
- Second Draft Report posted on the document information page

Step 3 – NFPA Technical Meeting

- Notice of Intent to Make a Motion (NITMAM) accepted (5 weeks) following the posting of Second Draft Report
- NITMAMs are reviewed and valid motions are certified by the Motions Committee for presentation at the NFPA Technical Meeting
- NFPA membership meets each June at the NFPA Technical Meeting to act on Standards with "Certified Amending Motions" (certified NITMAMs)
- Committee(s) vote on any successful amendments to the Technical Committee Reports made by the NFPA membership at the NFPA Technical Meeting

Step 4 – Council Appeals and Issuance of Standard

- Notification of intent to file an appeal to the Standards Council on Technical Meeting action must be filed within 20 days of the NFPA Technical Meeting
- Standards Council decides, based on all evidence, whether to issue the standard or to take other action

Notes:

1. Time periods are approximate; refer to published schedules for actual dates.
2. Annual revision cycle documents with certified amending motions take approximately 101 weeks to complete.
3. Fall revision cycle documents receiving certified amending motions take approximately 141 weeks to complete.

Committee Membership Classifications[1,2,3,4]

The following classifications apply to Committee members and represent their principal interest in the activity of the Committee.

1. M   *Manufacturer:* A representative of a maker or marketer of a product, assembly, or system, or portion thereof, that is affected by the standard.
2. U   *User:* A representative of an entity that is subject to the provisions of the standard or that voluntarily uses the standard.
3. IM *Installer/Maintainer:* A representative of an entity that is in the business of installing or maintaining a product, assembly, or system affected by the standard.
4. L   *Labor:* A labor representative or employee concerned with safety in the workplace.
5. RT *Applied Research/Testing Laboratory:* A representative of an independent testing laboratory or independent applied research organization that promulgates and/or enforces standards.
6. E   *Enforcing Authority:* A representative of an agency or an organization that promulgates and/or enforces standards.
7. I   *Insurance:* A representative of an insurance company, broker, agent, bureau, or inspection agency.
8. C   *Consumer:* A person who is or represents the ultimate purchaser of a product, system, or service affected by the standard, but who is not included in (2).
9. SE *Special Expert:* A person not representing (1) through (8) and who has special expertise in the scope of the standard or portion thereof.

NOTE 1: "Standard" connotes code, standard, recommended practice, or guide.

NOTE 2: A representative includes an employee.

NOTE 3: While these classifications will be used by the Standards Council to achieve a balance for Technical Committees, the Standards Council may determine that new classifications of member or unique interests need representation in order to foster the best possible Committee deliberations on any project. In this connection, the Standards Council may make such appointments as it deems appropriate in the public interest, such as the classification of "Utilities" in the National Electrical Code Committee.

NOTE 4: Representatives of subsidiaries of any group are generally considered to have the same classification as the parent organization.

Submitting Public Input / Public Comment Through the Online Submission System

Following publication of the current edition of an NFPA standard, the development of the next edition begins and the standard is open for Public Input.

Submit a Public Input

NFPA accepts Public Input on documents through our online submission system at www.nfpa.org. To use the online submission system:

- Choose a document from the List of NFPA codes & standards or filter by Development Stage for "codes accepting public input."
- Once you are on the document page, select the "Next Edition" tab.
- Choose the link "The next edition of this standard is now open for Public Input." You will be asked to sign in or create a free online account with NFPA before using this system.
- Follow the online instructions to submit your Public Input (see www.nfpa.org/publicinput for detailed instructions).
- Once a Public Input is saved or submitted in the system, it can be located on the "My Profile" page by selecting the "My Public Inputs/Comments/NITMAMs" section.

Submit a Public Comment

Once the First Draft Report becomes available there is a Public Comment period. Any objections or further related changes to the content of the First Draft must be submitted at the Comment Stage. To submit a Public Comment follow the same steps as previously explained for the submission of Public Input.

Other Resources Available on the Document Information Pages

Header: View document title and scope, access to our codes and standards or NFCSS subscription, and sign up to receive email alerts.

Current & Prior Editions	Research current and previous edition information.
Next Edition	Follow the committee's progress in the processing of a standard in its next revision cycle.
Technical Committee	View current committee rosters or apply to a committee.
Ask a Technical Question	For members, officials, and AHJs to submit standards questions to NFPA staff. Our Technical Questions Service provides a convenient way to receive timely and consistent technical assistance when you need to know more about NFPA standards relevant to your work.
News	Provides links to available articles and research and statistical reports related to our standards.
Purchase Products & Training	Discover and purchase the latest products and training.
Related Products	View related publications, training, and other resources available for purchase.

Information on the NFPA Standards Development Process

I. Applicable Regulations. The primary rules governing the processing of NFPA standards (codes, standards, recommended practices, and guides) are the NFPA *Regulations Governing the Development of NFPA Standards (Regs)*. Other applicable rules include NFPA *Bylaws*, NFPA *Technical Meeting Convention Rules*, NFPA *Guide for the Conduct of Participants in the NFPA Standards Development Process*, and the NFPA *Regulations Governing Petitions to the Board of Directors from Decisions of the Standards Council*. Most of these rules and regulations are contained in the *NFPA Standards Directory*. For copies of the *Directory*, contact Codes and Standards Administration at NFPA headquarters; all these documents are also available on the NFPA website at "www.nfpa.org/regs."

The following is general information on the NFPA process. All participants, however, should refer to the actual rules and regulations for a full understanding of this process and for the criteria that govern participation.

II. Technical Committee Report. The Technical Committee Report is defined as "the Report of the responsible Committee(s), in accordance with the Regulations, in preparation of a new or revised NFPA Standard." The Technical Committee Report is in two parts and consists of the First Draft Report and the Second Draft Report. (See *Regs* at Section 1.4.)

III. Step 1: First Draft Report. The First Draft Report is defined as "Part one of the Technical Committee Report, which documents the Input Stage." The First Draft Report consists of the First Draft, Public Input, Committee Input, Committee and Correlating Committee Statements, Correlating Notes, and Ballot Statements. (See *Regs* at 4.2.5.2 and Section 4.3.) Any objection to an action in the First Draft Report must be raised through the filing of an appropriate Comment for consideration in the Second Draft Report or the objection will be considered resolved. [See *Regs* at 4.3.1(b).]

IV. Step 2: Second Draft Report. The Second Draft Report is defined as "Part two of the Technical Committee Report, which documents the Comment Stage." The Second Draft Report consists of the Second Draft, Public Comments with corresponding Committee Actions and Committee Statements, Correlating Notes and their respective Committee Statements, Committee Comments, Correlating Revisions, and Ballot Statements. (See *Regs* at 4.2.5.2 and Section 4.4.) The First Draft Report and the Second Draft Report together constitute the Technical Committee Report. Any outstanding objection following the Second Draft Report must be raised through an appropriate Amending Motion at the NFPA Technical Meeting or the objection will be considered resolved. [See *Regs* at 4.4.1(b).]

V. Step 3a: Action at NFPA Technical Meeting. Following the publication of the Second Draft Report, there is a period during which those wishing to make proper Amending Motions on the Technical Committee Reports must signal their intention by submitting a Notice of Intent to Make a Motion (NITMAM). (See *Regs* at 4.5.2.) Standards that receive notice of proper Amending Motions (Certified Amending Motions) will be presented for action at the annual June NFPA Technical Meeting. At the meeting, the NFPA membership can consider and act on these Certified Amending Motions as well as Follow-up Amending Motions, that is, motions that become necessary as a result of a previous successful Amending Motion. (See 4.5.3.2 through 4.5.3.6 and Table 1, Columns 1-3 of *Regs* for a summary of the available Amending Motions and who may make them.) Any outstanding objection following action at an NFPA Technical Meeting (and any further Technical Committee consideration following successful Amending Motions, see *Regs* at 4.5.3.7 through 4.6.5) must be raised through an appeal to the Standards Council or it will be considered to be resolved.

VI. Step 3b: Documents Forwarded Directly to the Council. Where no NITMAM is received and certified in accordance with the *Technical Meeting Convention Rules*, the standard is forwarded directly to the Standards Council for action on issuance. Objections are deemed to be resolved for these documents. (See *Regs* at 4.5.2.5.)

VII. Step 4a: Council Appeals. Anyone can appeal to the Standards Council concerning procedural or substantive matters related to the development, content, or issuance of any document of the NFPA or on matters within the purview of the authority of the Council, as established by the *Bylaws* and as determined by the Board of Directors. Such appeals must be in written form and filed with the Secretary of the Standards Council (see *Regs* at Section 1.6). Time constraints for filing an appeal must be in accordance with 1.6.2 of the *Regs*. Objections are deemed to be resolved if not pursued at this level.

VIII. Step 4b: Document Issuance. The Standards Council is the issuer of all documents (see Article 8 of *Bylaws*). The Council acts on the issuance of a document presented for action at an NFPA Technical Meeting within 75 days from the date of the recommendation from the NFPA Technical Meeting, unless this period is extended by the Council (see *Regs* at 4.7.2). For documents forwarded directly to the Standards Council, the Council acts on the issuance of the document at its next scheduled meeting, or at such other meeting as the Council may determine (see *Regs* at 4.5.2.5 and 4.7.4).

IX. Petitions to the Board of Directors. The Standards Council has been delegated the responsibility for the administration of the codes and standards development process and the issuance of documents. However, where extraordinary circumstances requiring the intervention of the Board of Directors exist, the Board of Directors may take any action necessary to fulfill its obligations to preserve the integrity of the codes and standards development process and to protect the interests of the NFPA. The rules for petitioning the Board of Directors can be found in the *Regulations Governing Petitions to the Board of Directors from Decisions of the Standards Council* and in Section 1.7 of the *Regs*.

X. For More Information. The program for the NFPA Technical Meeting (as well as the NFPA website as information becomes available) should be consulted for the date on which each report scheduled for consideration at the meeting will be presented. To view the First Draft Report and Second Draft Report as well as information on NFPA rules and for up-to-date information on schedules and deadlines for processing NFPA documents, check the NFPA website (www.nfpa.org/docinfo) or contact NFPA Codes & Standards Administration at (617) 984-7246.